HABITATS OF THE WORLD

FRESHWATER HABITATS

ALISON BALLANCE

MW00436409

Streams and Rivers 2

The Amazon River 4

Ponds and Lakes 6

Lake Baikal 8

Wetlands 10

Freshwater Animal Life 12

Freshwater Plant Life 18

Freshwater Food 22

Glossary 24

Index .24

Dominie Press, Inc.

Streams and Rivers

Streams begin life as drops of rain. When rain falls high in the mountains, it begins to flow downhill and become streams. Little streams join to make big streams. When big streams come together, they become rivers. The water in streams and rivers is always moving.

The Amazon River

The Amazon River, in South America, is the biggest river in the world. It carries more water than any other river. The Amazon flows for more than 4,000 miles before it reaches the sea.

Ponds and Lakes

Ponds and lakes form when **fresh water** fills up **hollows**. Hollows are sunken areas in the ground, such as small valleys. The water in a pond or lake is always **still**. Water in a **shallow** pond can get very warm. Water in a deep lake is often cold.

Lake Baikal

Lake Baikal, in Siberia, is more than 5,000 feet deep. It is the deepest lake in the world. It contains nearly a quarter of all the world's fresh water. Rare freshwater seals live in the waters of Lake Baikal.

Wetlands

Wetlands are places where land and water meet. Bogs, marshes, and swamps are different kinds of wetlands. The Everglades, in Florida, form a giant swamp. This area is rich in wildlife. Alligators, crocodiles, and **exotic**, colorful birds live in the Everglades.

Freshwater Animal Life

Frogs lay their eggs in shallow water. The eggs hatch into tadpoles, which swim and breathe under water like fish. Tadpoles turn into frogs.

Dragonflies start their lives under water. At this stage of their lives, they are called nymphs. Dragonfly nymphs are fierce hunters. Nymphs become adult dragonflies that have wings and can fly.

Many birds feed in lakes and rivers. Some birds dive below the water's surface to catch fish. Other birds eat plants. When ducks look for food, they put their heads under water.

Freshwater Plant Life

It is hard for plants to grow in flowing water. They often get swept away. It is easier for plants to grow in still water. Some plants, such as water lilies, float on the surface of the water.

Freshwater plants called rushes live on the muddy edges of ponds and lakes. As they grow, their roots and stems trap more and more mud. As a pond gets older, it fills with mud and rushes. Then the pond slowly turns into land.

Freshwater Food

Freshwater habitats are very important to people as well as plants and animals. Rice, which is the main food for people living in Asia, is one example of this. Rice is grown in fields called **paddies**. The paddies are flooded with fresh water.

We need fresh water and freshwater habitats to **survive**.

GLOSSARY

exotic:	Unusual; fascinating; strange
fresh water:	Water that is not salty
freshwater habitats:	Areas where fresh water can be found
hollows:	Sunken areas in the land, such as small valleys
paddies:	Rice fields
shallow:	Not very deep
still:	Not moving
survive:	To stay alive
wetlands:	Bogs, marshes, and swamps

INDEX

alligators, 11
Amazon River, 5
Asia, 23
birds, 11, 17
bogs, 11
crocodiles, 11
dragonflies, 15
ducks, 17
eggs, 13
Everglades, 11
fish, 13, 17
Florida, 11
food, 17, 23

freshwater seals, 9
frogs, 13
hollows, 7
Lake Baikal, 9
lake(s), 7, 9, 17, 21
marshes, 11
nymphs, 15
paddies, 23
plants, 17, 19, 21, 23
ponds, 7, 21
rain, 3
rice, 23
river(s), 3, 5, 17

roots, 21
rushes, 21
sea, 5
Siberia, 9
South America, 5
stems, 21
streams, 3
swamp(s), 11
tadpoles, 13
valleys, 7
water lilies, 19
wetlands, 11
wildlife, 11
wings, 15